HAUSALAND

HAUSALAND

THE FORTRESS KINGDOMS

PHILIP KOSLOW

CHELSEA HOUSE PUBLISHERS • New York • Philadelphia

Frontispiece: The remains of an elaborate Hausa fortification near Zinder, in the Niger Republic.

On the Cover: An artist's rendering of a terra-cotta head from Nok in central Nigeria; in the background, a view of the cloth-dyeing pits in Kano, the leading city of Hausaland.

CHELSEA HOUSE PUBLISHERS
Editorial Director Richard Rennert
Executive Managing Editor Karyn Gullen Browne
Copy Chief Robin James
Picture Editor Adrian G. Allen
Art Director Robert Mitchell
Manufacturing Director Gerald Levine
Assistant Art Director Joan Ferrigno

THE KINGDOMS OF AFRICA
Senior Editor Martin Schwabacher

Staff for HAUSALAND
Editorial Assistant Sydra Mallery
Designer Cambraia Magalhães
Picture Researcher Pat Burns
Cover Illustrator Bradford Brown

First Printing
1 3 5 7 9 8 6 4 2

Library of Congress Cataloging-in-Publication Data

Koslow, Philip.
  Hausaland: the fortress kingdoms / Philip Koslow.
     p. cm.—(The Kingdoms of Africa)
Includes bibliographical references and index.
   ISBN   0-7910-3130.
              0-7910-2945-X (pbk.)
    1. Hausa (African People)—History—Juvenile literature. [1.Hausa (African people)] I. Title.
II. Series.   94-31093
DT515.45.H38K68 1995   CIP
960'.04937—dc20   AC

CONTENTS

Titles In
THE KINGDOMS OF AFRICA

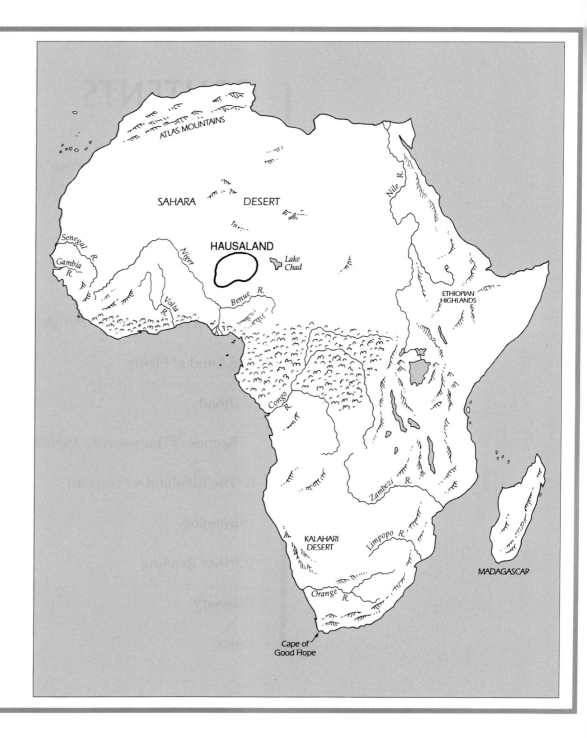

"CIVILIZATION AND MAGNIFICENCE"

On a sunny morning in July 1796, Mungo Park, a Scottish doctor turned explorer, achieved a major goal of his long and difficult trek through West Africa when he reached the banks of the mighty Niger River. Along the river was a cluster of four large towns, which together made up the city of Segu, the principal settlement of the Bambara people. The sight of Segu dazzled Park as much as the spectacle of the broad, shining waterway. "The view of this extensive city," he wrote, "the numerous canoes upon the river; the crowded population; and the cultivated state of the surrounding country, formed altogether a prospect of civilization and magnificence, which I little expected to find in the bosom of Africa."

Park's account of his journey, *Travels in the Interior Districts of Africa*, became a best-seller in England. But his positive reflections on Africa were soon brushed aside by the English and other Europeans, who were engaged in a profitable trade in slaves along the West African coast and were eventually to carve up the entire continent into colonies. Later explorers such as Richard Burton, who spoke of the "childishness" and "backward-ness" of Africans, achieved more lasting fame than did Park, who drowned during a second expedition to Africa in 1806. Thus it is not surprising that 100 years after Park's arrival at Segu, a professor at England's Oxford University could write with bland self-assurance that African history before the arrival of Europeans had been nothing more than "blank, uninteresting, brutal barbarism." The professor's opinion was published when the British Empire was at its height, and it represented a point of view that was necessary to justify the exploitation of Africans. If, as the professor claimed, Africans had lived in a state of chaos throughout their history, then their European conquerors

7

A relief map of Africa indicating the territory of Hausaland.

could believe that they were doing a noble deed by imposing their will and their way of life upon Africa.

The colonialist view of African history held sway into the 20th century. But as the century progressed, more enlightened scholars began to take a fresh look at the African past. As archaeologists (scientists who study the physical remains of past societies) explored the sites of former African cities, they found that Africans had enjoyed a high level of civilization hundreds of years before the arrival of Europeans. In many respects, the kingdoms and cities of Africa had been equal to or more advanced than European societies during the same period.

Modern scientists also reject the idea—fostered by Europeans during the time of the slave trade and colonialism—that there is any connection between a people's skin color and their capacity for achievement and self-government. Differences in pigmentation, scientists now recognize, are based solely upon climate and have nothing to do with intellectual ability. When the human species began to develop in the torrid regions of Africa some 7.5 million years ago, humans were all dark skinned because dark pigmentation protected them from the harmful ultraviolet rays of the sun. However, when humans later migrated from Africa to colder climates where there was far less sunlight, heavy pigmentation became a drawback—it prevented the skin from absorbing the amount of sunlight needed to produce vitamin D, which is essential for the growth of bones and teeth. Hence lighter skin began to predominate in

Mungo Park (1771–1806) was among the earliest Europeans to provide a detailed account of West Africa. His 1799 book Travels in the Interior Districts of Africa *remains a classic in the literature of exploration.*

8

Europe, with the peoples of Asia, the Middle East, and North Africa occupying a middle ground between Europeans and the darker-skinned Africans. Rather than being a sign of superiority, lighter skin can therefore be seen as a divergence from the original skin color of all human beings.

As early as 400 B.C., a West African people centered in the village of Nok, in present-day Nigeria, produced small sculptures that are equal in workmanship and beauty to anything created by the widely acclaimed artists of ancient Greece and Rome. By A.D. 750, the kingdom of ancient Ghana, also known as the Land of Gold, was flourishing in West Africa. When Ghana began to decline in the 12th century, power shifted to the empire of Mali, and Mali was in turn supplanted by Songhay and Kanem-Borno. The history of both Songhay and Kanem-Borno was closely intertwined with another significant force—the fortress kingdoms of Hausaland.

A terra-cotta head produced by the Nok culture of central Nigeria. As early as 400 B.C., the sculptors of Nok produced works of art that rank among the world's great masterpieces.

9

Chapter 1 | THE SNAKE KILLER

According to the main legend of the Hausa people (pronounced HOW-sa), there was once a prince named Bayajida, who lived in the city of Baghdad in the Middle East but decided to leave home after quarreling with his father. He traveled west to the kingdom of Borno near Lake Chad in West Africa. At first he was welcomed by the king of Borno and married the king's daughter. But soon the king began to fear that Bayajida would become too powerful and take the throne. The king plotted to murder his son-in-law, but Bayajida's wife discovered the plot, and she and Bayajida fled. They soon reached a town called Garun Gabas, where Bayajida's wife gave birth to a child. Bayajida was forced to leave his wife and child behind as he continued to travel west. Eventually, he reached

The old city walls of Katsina rise above the typically flat landscape of Hausaland in Nigeria. Hausa traditions indicate that Katsina was founded more than 1,000 years ago by Kumayau, the son of a powerful Hausa king named Bawogari.

Daura in what is now the northeast part of Hausaland.

In Daura, Bayajida found lodging in the house of an old woman named Waira. When Bayajida asked his landlady for some water, she replied that the people of Daura could get water only on Fridays because the town well was guarded by a giant snake. Bayajida was determined to get water all the same, so he took Waira's bucket and went to the well. As soon as Bayajida lowered the bucket, the snake, whose name was Sarki, rose out of the well and attacked him. Drawing his sword, Bayajida cut off Sarki's head and hid it. Then he drew his water and retired for the night.

The following morning, the townspeople were astounded to find Sarki's massive, headless body hanging out of the well. When the queen of Daura heard the news, she rushed to the scene with her warriors and offered half the town as a reward to the person who had killed the snake. Many of the townspeople came forward to claim credit for the deed, but none of them could produce Sarki's head as proof. Finally, Waira spoke up and said that the young man who had lodged with her the night before had somehow managed to get water from the well; she thought that he might have killed the snake. The townspeople sent for Bayajida, who told of his deed and then produced the head of the snake. The queen then offered him half the town, but Bayajida suggested that she marry him instead. The queen agreed.

Bayajida took up residence in the palace and was given the title Makas-Sarki, or Snake Killer. Bayajida and the queen of Daura had a son named Bawogari, who became the ruler of Daura after the death of his parents. Bawogari's first son, Gazaura, followed him as ruler of Daura. Bawogari had five more sons, and each one went off on his own to found a separate state. Bagauda founded Kano; Gunguma founded Zaria; Duma founded Gobir; Kumayau founded Katsina; and Zuma Kogi, the youngest, founded Rano. A seventh kingdom, Garun Gabas, was ruled by the son that Bayajida had with his first wife, the princess of Borno. Thus the seven original states of Hausaland, known in the Hausa language as the *hausa bakwai*—Daura, Kano, Zaria, Katsina, Gobir, Rano, and Garun Gabas—came into being.

While in Daura, Bayajida also had a son named Karbogari with his concubine (a gift from the queen). Karbogari's sons established seven more states: Kebbi, Zamfara, Gwari, Kwararafa, Yoruba, Nupe, and Yamuri. These are the lesser Hausa states, which are known as the *banza bakwai*, or "unworthy seven."

In the early days of African historical research, a number of historians concluded from the Bayajida legend that the Hausa originally came to West Africa from the Middle East. Most modern scholars reject this theory and believe instead that the Hausa originated in their present homeland. According to this view, the Hausa are the descendants of the peoples who fished on the western shores of Lake Chad, which was once a vast inland sea more than twice its present size. When the climate of Africa began to dry out about 4,000 years ago, Lake Chad began to shrink, and the Hausa pushed westward. Wherever they settled, they cleared away forest and brush so that they could plant crops and raise cattle, sheep, and goats. Thus there were Hausa in Hausaland long before the 14 city-states came into existence.

Viewed in this light, the Bayajida legend lends itself to an alternate historical interpretation: though the Hausa people were long established in Hausaland, the first rulers of the Hausa city-states were outsiders, most likely from the Lake Chad region. Because they possessed horses and iron weapons, the newcomers were able to gain dominance over the farmers and herders of Hausaland. These conquerors took the rank of *sarki* (plural *sarkuna*) as a shortened form of Bayajida's title. The sarkuna may have been related to the lighter-skinned Berber tribes of the Sahara or the peoples of the Nile Valley; in any case, they married Hausa women and their descendants were absorbed into the Hausa stock.

The legend's claim that two sets of seven states were founded at once is probably more symbolic than historically accurate; numerous cultures throughout history have believed that the number seven contains some special power. It is far more likely, as Roland Oliver and Brian Fagan assert in *Africa in the Iron Age*, that the Hausa states came into being gradually, during a long-term search

13

A sculpture of a man with a snake wrapped around his body, created by a West African artist in the 14th century. According to a widespread legend, the Hausa states owe their origin to the prince Bayajida, who killed a giant snake that was terrorizing the people of Daura.

A herd of elephants on the shores of Lake Chad, as depicted in a 19th-century engraving. Historians believe that the ancestors of the Hausa people inhabited the shores of Lake Chad thousands of years ago and migrated westward during a prolonged dry period.

14

for sources of underground water that favored the development of large-scale agriculture. Successful planting led to population growth, and the Hausa city-states emerged from this fortunate combination.

The British scholar H. A. S. Johnston, who studied Hausa literature and folk-lore during the 1950s, has given the following description of Hausaland, which extends from Aïr in the Sahara to the southern forest belt and from the Lake Chad region to the Niger Valley:

It is a land of rolling plains which stretch away in every direction to apparently limitless horizons. It has no mountains and few hills. Its towns and villages nestle in the valleys where water is plentiful and the soil fertile. Round them cultivation has cleared away the bush and left the land open but studded with fine trees like an English park. The intervening heights, by contrast, are still well clothed in bush which sometimes rolls away as far as the eye can reach. Only occasionally does a black granite inselberg [outcropping of rock] or a range of red laterite hills, a shallow river with wide sandy banks, or a considerable town of flat-roofed houses, encircled perhaps by a great mud wall . . . appear to give variety to the scene. . . . The picture is saved from monotony by the extraordinary changes which the seasons bring about. In March, when there has already been a drought for five or six months, the hot weather arrives. The sun then shines fiercely out of the brassy sky and dust-devils [small whirlwinds] stalk across the parched landscape. But by July the rains will have transformed the scene: there will now be a soft wind coming from the south-west and the country will be looking as green as Ireland. Four months later, however, by November, another transformation will have taken place. The Harmattan [a strong desert wind] will then be blowing out of the north-east, bringing crisp days and chilly nights, and the landscape will have resumed the tawny coloring which is the real livery of Africa.

Johnston points out that these surroundings have had a powerful effect on the history of the Hausa. Because of the fertility of the land during the rainy season, Hausa farmers could obtain a year's provisions with only six months of labor, leaving the rest of the year—the dry season—for other pursuits, both peaceful and warlike. It was these pursuits that created the compelling drama of Hausa history.

15

اللهم صل على سيدنا محمد
عدد ما في علم الله صلاة
دائمة بدوام ملك الله
ثلاثا
ابتدا الثلث
الثاني
كاشف الكرب صلى الله عليه وسلم
رافع الرتب صلى الله عليه وسلم
صاحب الفرج صلى الله عليه

Chapter 2 | "STAND FIRM"

The Hausa city-states began to develop in the northeastern part of Hausaland around the year 1000. Much of the information about these early years is contained in a Hausa document entitled the *Kano Chronicle*. Though written at the end of the 19th century, the chronicle clearly draws upon the oral traditions that have been handed down through the centuries. The words of the *Kano Chronicle* are Hausa, even though the written characters are Arabic. Because the languages of West Africa were purely oral, those peoples who wished to preserve their traditions in writing eventually adopted the alphabets of other languages.

The *Kano Chronicle* reaches back even further than the legend of Daura, tracing Kano's history to Dala, "a black man of great stature and might, a hunter, who slew elephants with his stick and carried them on his head about nine miles." The great hunter and his family settled on the hill of Dala and built a shrine to their god, Tchunburburai. Dala's descendants ruled the area around the hill until Bagauda, the grandson of Bayajida, conquered them and destroyed the sacred grove of Tchunburburai. According to the chronicle, Bagauda began to erect a fortified city around the hill of Dala, and he ruled as sarki from 999 to 1063.

The process of building Kano was a gradual one. The earthen wall encircling the city was not completed until the reign of the fifth sarki, Tsaraki, who ruled from 1136 to 1194. Following the distinctive Hausa city design, the buildings filled barely half of the area enclosed by the walls. Apart from the hill of Dala and a

This Hausa version of the Koran, the holy book of Islam, dates from the late 17th or early 18th century. The words have been translated from Arabic into Hausa, but the Arabic alphabet has been retained—this form of writing is known in Hausaland as ajami.

second hill of the same size (about 200 feet high), the rest of the city consisted of open fields. This open space served two purposes: it allowed people from the surrounding country to take shelter in times of war, and it provided land for growing crops so that the residents of Kano could not be starved into submission by a besieging army.

Such precautions were never out of place, because like many regions of the world during that era, Hausaland was the scene of frequent warfare. Like rulers everywhere, the sarkuna of Kano and the other Hausa cities were always trying to increase their domains and their wealth. The sarkuna often launched military raids against their neighbors, bringing home captives who were put to work in the fields or sold to North African slave traders. In other cases, dominance could be gained by peaceful means; neighboring peoples would provide tribute to a sarki in the form of goods or would voluntarily offer slaves, in return for protection against raiders and other invaders.

The sarkuna varied in their eagerness to employ military force. When Kano's sarki Shekkaru (1290–1307) was confronted by a group of peasants who did not wish to be controlled by Kano, his advisers urged him to use force: "If you try to make peace with the people they will say that you are afraid. . . . We will fight them, and if we prevail over them we will cut the throats of all their chief men and destroy their god." However, Shekkaru chose to meet with his adversaries. They brought him presents and said, "If the domains of a ruler are wide, he should be patient; if they are not so, he will not obtain possession of the whole country by impatience." Shekkaru was moved by these words and allowed the country people to retain their independence. His son Barandamasu, on the other hand, was a man who in the words of the chronicle "excelled all men in courage, dignity, impetuosity in war, vindictiveness and strength." Bolstered by nine warriors "who were equal to a thousand," he routed the worshipers of the god Tchibiri, destroyed their sacred tree, and compelled them to reveal the god's secret so that he could possess Tchibiri's power. The chronicle also indicates that during Barandamasu's reign (1307–43), the *kakaki* (three-foot-long trumpets) first came into use in Kano, along with a national anthem, whose words were "Stand firm, Kano is your city."

The struggle between the sarkuna and their neighbors was essentially a conflict between rulers and ruled rather

18

than a religious clash. However, by the time of Shekkaru, the issue of worship had taken on a new dimension in Hausaland. Now there was no longer merely a conflict between competing African gods. A completely different form of worship had penetrated Hausaland from the outside—the religion of Islam.

Islam arose in the deserts of Arabia, to the east of Africa. The inhabitants of Arabia, who were mainly farmers and wandering herders, had for centuries worshiped a variety of gods and spirits, many of them associated with forces of nature. As they honored these age-old beliefs, however, the Arabians were in close contact with peoples who practiced newer religions, such as Judaism and Christianity. Judaism and Christianity were based upon worship of a single god. Both religions had been founded by powerful figures who had experienced what they believed to be a direct communication from God, revealing a great truth for all humanity.

The prophet who emerged to express a new religious idea in Arabia was named Muhammad. Born in the city of Mecca in 570, Muhammad spent his youth as a camel driver and then became a tradesman. At the age of 40, he had a vision of a faith based on the worship of a single

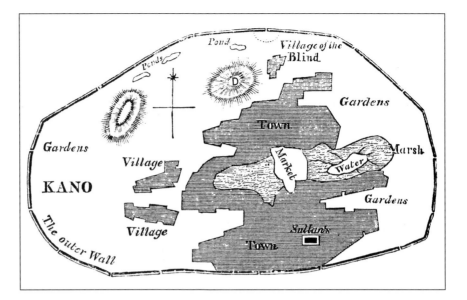

god, Allah, who demanded strict devotion, regular prayer, and pure habits in return for eternal salvation. Muhammad quickly attracted a group of followers, but he also aroused bitter opposition among the Arabian tribespeople, who felt that he was attacking their traditional beliefs and way of life. In 622, Muhammad's enemies forced him to leave Mecca and resettle in Medina. There he continued to gather converts, who became known as Muslims, and to develop the principles that grew into the religion of Islam. By the time of Muhammad's death in 632, his powerful influence had spread throughout Arabia. His teachings

A 19th-century plan of Kano, with the Hill of Dala, the original settlement, marked by a D. Access to the city was provided by 15 fortified gates.

19

20

were recorded in the holy book known as the Koran, which has the same importance for Muslims as the Old Testament has for Jews and the New Testament has for Christians.

Muhammad's followers, led by the prophet's father-in-law Abu Bakr, set out to spread their faith and culture. By 645, Muslim warriors had conquered all of Arabia and much of the Middle East. From there they moved westward into the central part of North Africa. By the end of the 7th century, the Muslims had ex-

tended their power to the Atlantic coast of Africa, and shortly afterward they crossed the Strait of Gibraltar to conquer much of present-day Spain and Portugal.

Despite their warlike zeal, the Muslims did not attempt to conquer West Africa or impose their beliefs at the point of a sword. They would have found it extremely difficult, if not impossible, to maintain military supply routes and communications across the Sahara, and in any case they had more to gain from maintaining friendly trade relations with the peoples of the Sudan (the Arabic term for sub-Saharan Africa was *Bilad al-Sudan,* "the land of the black peoples").

Nations to the west, east, and south of Hausaland began feelng the influence of Islam in the 11th century, as their rulers and leading merchants adopted the new faith. Takrur and Ghana in the West, Mali in the South, and Kanem-Borno in the East were all officially Muslim states by the 14th century. In many cases, the change of religion was a matter of convenience rather than belief, designed to foster better relations with the traders bringing valuable goods from North Africa. Islam was generally confined to the royal courts and the major trading centers. The people of the countryside continued to follow their tradi-

Muhammad and his family, as depicted in a 17th-century Islamic manuscript. Following his death in 632, Muhammad's followers spread the religion of Islam throughout the Middle East and North Africa.

tional religions, which had much in common with the pre-Islamic beliefs of the Arabian tribespeople. Living in a challenging environment and depending for their survival on the fertility of the land and the bounty of the waters, the country people regarded the forces of nature with religious awe. Many of their rituals were intended to appease the spirits of the sky, earth, and water; a number of animals, such as the snake and the ram, were also considered sacred. Though many West Africans honored a supreme being or creator god, the notion of a single deity such as Allah or Jehovah, all-powerful yet removed from the earth and its teeming life, was quite foreign to their thinking. They also had little sympathy for the Islamic idea that a person's spirit departs from the earth after death, passing on to receive reward in heaven or torment in hell. West Africans, by contrast, believed that their ancestors' spirits remained in the world, as would their own, and that the dead would live again in future generations.

Hausaland began trade relations with North Africa as early as the 12th century. But because the Hausa lived in independent city-states and did not have a centralized kingdom like some of their West African neighbors, Islam's progress

in Hausaland was bound to be slower—there was no supreme ruler whose conversion could dramatically bring a new religion into vogue. Nevertheless, Islamic teachers and holy men, known in Hausaland as *malams*, regularly accompanied trading caravans from North Africa and did their best to convince West Africans that Allah could bring them greater benefits than their own gods.

In the time of the sarki Yaji (1349–85), Muslims made their presence felt in more direct ways. When Yaji was waging war against the neighboring city of Santolo, a party of Wangara Muslims came to Hausaland from the kingdom of Mali. The Wangara (black Africans known as expert traders) offered to take part in the attack on Santolo—but only if Yaji agreed to adopt their religion. According to the chronicle, "The Sarki commanded every town in Kano country to observe the times of prayer. . . . A mosque was built beneath the sacred tree facing east [in the direction of Mecca], and prayers were made at the five appointed times in it." When Yaji conquered Santolo and then Warji, he became the first sarki to bring all the surrounding countryside under the control of Kano. His victory also ensured that Islam would be the official religion of Kano's domains.

Chapter 3 | THE FORTRESS KINGDOMS

In this portrayal of West African troops in action, the charging cavalrymen and their mounts wear the quilted armor that appeared in Hausaland during the 15th century. Throughout much of their history, the Hausa states battled one another for control of important trade routes.

By the 15th century, all seven Hausa bakwai had emerged on the West African scene as full-fledged city-states profiting from the trade between the Sudan and North Africa. Katsina, Kano's closest neighbor, became a major power during the reign of Muhammad Korau (1145–95). The Nigerian scholar Mahdi Amadu, writing in volume 4 of the *UNESCO General History of Africa,* has described the process by which Katsina grew from a mere settlement to a state:

> While still at Durbi [the seat of his chiefdom], Korau identified an important meeting-point of several trade routes, the site of an iron-mine and an important shrine, known as Bawada; and as *sarki,* he established there a new walled city (*birni*) called Katsina. . . . The new settlement soon became attractive to both settlers and passing traders, and thus brought more power and wealth to its ruler. Little by little, the surrounding chiefs came to pay him tributes in the form of iron bars. . . . With such a strong economic and political base, Muhammad Korau began to raid far and wide, until he had carved for himself a large domain, the kingdom of Katsina.

A similar pattern prevailed in the development of Zaria, to the south of Kano and Katsina. Zaria emerged when Barkwa, the ruler of Turunku, seized the nearby city of Kufina. Barkwa then built a new capital on the outskirts of Kufina and named the city Zaria after one of his daughters. Zaria then began to expand southward through a series of military campaigns. According to the *Kano Chronicle,* one of

24

the state's greatest military leaders was Zaria's sister Amina, who assumed the title *magajiya* (queen) in 1576 and ruled until her death in 1610.

Amina was a formidable character. As a young princess she had many suitors, including the emir of Kano, who reportedly sent her 100 slaves and 50 bags of cloth in a vain attempt to win her heart. Rather than serving an important man, Amina wished to be a powerful force in her own right, and she fulfilled her ambitions. The *Kano Chronicle* indicates that she led her armies as far south as Nupe and Kwararafa, extending the borders of Zaria to the confluence of the Niger and Benue rivers. Amina is said to have built a walled camp wherever she halted in her military expeditions: as S. J. Hogben and A. H. M. Kirk-Greene explain in *The Emirates of Northern Nigeria,* "Thus it is that in many parts of Hausaland ancient town walls are called *ganuwar Amina,* 'Amina's walls,' even though they were not necessarily built by her." Examining other accounts of Amina's exploits, the authors continue: "Whether Amina married is still disputed in Zaria history, but tradition certainly credits her with taking a lover in every town she conquered; but as camp was broken on the following morning, her brief bridegroom was beheaded so that none should live to tell the tale. . . . Her praise is sung: 'Amina, daughter of Nikatau, a woman as capable as a man' (*kallabi tsakanin rawuna*)."

During Amina's time the states of Gobir, Rano, Zamfara, and Kebbi also emerged as typical Hausa communities surrounded by sturdy mud walls. Hausa society was complex and well organized. The cities were divided into wards, and the wards were further divided into family compounds, each headed by an elder. The leader of each ward was responsible for repairing a different section of the city wall, which would normally suffer some damage during the rainy season. The repair work was performed at the end of the harvest and the onset of the dry season. Only when the city's rulers were satisfied that the walls were in good condition could the men of the city turn to their crafts, organize trading caravans, or go off on raids.

Meanwhile, Kano itself continued to prosper and to lead Hausaland in political innovation. The most powerful sarkuna in this period were Abdullah Burja and Muhammad Rumfa. Abdullah Burja, who ruled from 1438 to 1452, was reputedly the first person in Kano to own camels and is credited with opening the road to Gwanja, which lay at the edge of the

(Continued on page 29)

HAUSA ARCHITECTURE

During the yearly dry season (November to March), the Hausa take the opportunity to build new houses and repair walls that have been damaged by the spring and summer rains. The traditional method of building employs mud bricks manufactured from the red laterite soil that predominates in Hausaland. The construction of an average-sized mud-brick house requires about three months.

This house in Kano shows the typical features of Hausa architecture. Mud bricks can be seen at the base of the front wall on the right, where the exterior plaster has worn away. When the plaster was originally applied, the builders created the delicate patterns on two of the walls by running their fingers over the surface.

A group of houses in Kano. Structural beams, such as those protruding from the house at the right, are usually cut from native palm trees, several of which rise in the background.

A traditional hut in a Hausa village exemplifies the original style of West African architecture, which features circular walls and conical thatched roofs. The tightly woven thatch is completely waterproof, even during the torrential downpours of the rainy season.

28

An interior view of the palace that houses the emir of Argungu, a city on the Kebbi River. Hausa palaces typically include guest quarters, reception rooms, family compounds, stables, and barracks. The largest palaces extend over more than 30 acres and provide shelter for as many as 1,000 persons.

(Continued from page 24)

southern forest belt. Both developments contributed greatly to the growing prosperity of Kano. The possession of camels gave the merchants of Kano the ability to take their goods across the Sahara rather than having to wait for North Africans to come south. Contact with Gwanja gave Kano access to gold dust and kola nuts from the forest belt. (Kolas, which contain a stimulant similar to caffeine, were in great demand throughout Africa.) In order to attract traders, Abdullah Burja established the Kurmi Market, which soon became one of the leading commercial centers of the Sudan. At this time, Hausa traders began to rival the Wangara as traveling merchants, spreading both Islam and Hausa culture. As a result, Hausa now rivals Swahili as the most widely spoken language in Africa.

Abdullah Burja also employed Kano's military forces to great advantage, acquiring numerous slaves in raids against the peoples to the south: at one point, the sarki commanded 21,000 slaves, distributed among 21 settlements. Led by Daud, Kano's *galadima* (chief minister), Kano's forces were now equipped with *lifidi*, quilted armor that protected the cavalry's horses. The horsemen themselves wore plumed iron helmets and chain mail (flexible body armor made by linking thousands of small iron rings). These military innovations were most likely imported into Hausaland from nearby Kanem-Borno, whose rulers had enjoyed stunning success in war.

Kano's 20th sarki, Muhammad Rumfa (1463–99), is credited by the *Kano Chronicle* with building a new palace, extending the walls of the city, and improving Kano's defenses. He also increased the splendor of his royal court, patterning himself on the Muslim rulers of the North and the East. For example, he maintained a harem of 1,000 wives, equipped his attendants with ostrich-feather fans (*figini*), and instituted splendid festivities to mark Muslim holy days. On a more practical level, Muhammad Rumfa took measures to make the government of Kano more efficient. The city had grown to a point where no ruler could effectively manage its affairs on his own, so Muhammad Rumfa installed a nine member council known as the *tara-ta-Kano* (the Kano nine) to assist him in making major governmental decisions. In the past, the leading officials were drawn from the clans, or descent lines, that had played a leading role in the development of the city. Muhammad Rumfa continued this tradition—he could hardly have maintained the loyalty of his leading subjects other-

29

wise—but he also appointed people of more humble birth, many of them slaves, to manage the treasury, staff the palace and city guard, and oversee the harem.

This practice indicates that slavery in West Africa was quite different from the slavery that Africans later endured in the Americas. Though the life of a slave in Kano, Songhay, or Kanem-Borno was hardly enviable, Africans did not believe that their slaves were inferior beings. Slaves were people who had to serve oth-

ers because they had been defeated in war; those who proved to be loyal and capable had the opportunity to better their lot in a variety of ways. Eunuchs (slaves who had been castrated by their conquerors) were particularly valued as government officials. Because the eunuchs could not begin descent lines of their own, they would not harbor ambitions for their own children as other officials might. By appointing officials whose principal loyalty was to the state or the ruler, leaders such as Muhammad Rumfa developed a structure comparable to the civil service of modern nations.

Ultimately, the prosperity of all the communities of West Africa depended upon agriculture. Hausaland was blessed with especially fertile soil that yielded a surplus of food for the populace and a generous supply of cotton for Hausaland's textile industries. The Hausa carefully organized the activity of farming. As Mahdi Amadu has explained, "The farmers (*talakawa*, sing. *talaka*) were directed in their agricultural activities by a leader—*sarkin poma* (chief of crops)—who was responsible for closely watching for the onset of the rainy season and for making appropriate sacrifices to local gods in order to ensure a good harvest. . . . In the course of time, three kinds of farms developed in

A map of the major Hausa states and cities. In times of war, the numerous fortified settlements of Hausaland provided refuge for the people of the surrounding countryside.

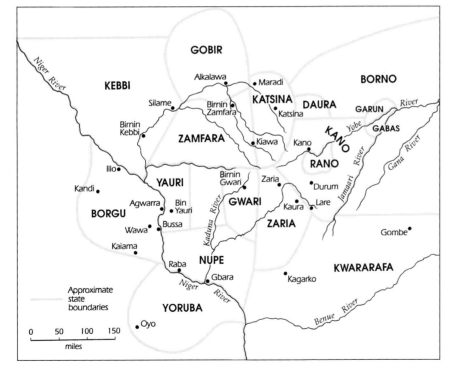

30

A group of traders and their camels rest at an oasis in the Sahara Desert. Each year, after gathering their harvest, the Hausa engaged in commerce with other regions of Africa—as a result, Hausa culture and language gained influence far beyond the borders of Hausaland.

31

Hausaland: *gandum sarkin,* the king's field, characterized by its large size; *gandum gide,* the family field . . . and lastly *gayauna* or *gayamma,* the individual field. Slave labor played a major role on the *gandum sarkin* as well as on the large estates of the state dignitaries."

By the early 17th century, when an Arab traveler known as Leo Africanus visited Hausaland, the prosperity of the country was overwhelmingly obvious. Leo noted the abundance of corn, rice, and cotton growing in the fields. He also wrote of the "wild, woody mountains containing many springs of water. In these woods grow plenty of wild citrons and lemons, which differ not much in taste from the best of all. In the midst of this province [Kano] stands a town of the same name, the walls and houses whereof are built for the most part of a kind of chalk [the typical clay of West Africa]. The inhabitants are rich merchants and most civil people." Hausaland seemingly had reached an ideal stage of development, but there were many challenges still to come.

Chapter 4 | A LAND OF PLENTY

As the Hausa states grew in wealth and strength, they played an increasingly important role in the African economy, serving as collection points for goods passing back and forth between the southern and northern coasts. At the same time, Hausaland also became an increasingly attractive prize for ambitious neighbors. "It is the hen with chicks that fears the hawk," a Hausa proverb runs, and by the 16th century the hawks were descending. In the West, Songhay was expanding rapidly under its great leader Askia Muhammad. After conquering the lands along the Niger, Songhay's troops pushed deep into Hausaland. They exerted so much pressure on the Hausa states that a number of sarkuna were forced to pay Askia Muhammad a yearly tribute in the form of slaves.

The spired corners and ornate wall design of this house in Kano are typical features of Hausa architecture.

The arrangement between Songhay and the Hausa states was clearly not a stable one, because Daud, one of Askia Muhammad's sons, felt the need to launch a raid on Katsina in 1554. Daud apparently had little respect for Katsina's army, because he sent only 24 horsemen against the city. The *Tarikh al-Sudan*, a 17th-century Songhay chronicle, described the outcome of the battle between these horsemen and some 400 Katsina cavalry:

> The Katsina people killed 15 of their enemy. . . . They took the remaining nine, all of whom were wounded, prisoner. . . . The victors took care of the wounded and gave them the greatest attention. Then they set them at liberty and sent them back to Askia Daud, telling them that "men of such quality, endowed with such great

valor and such courage, did not deserve to die." The vigor and daring of these warriors so amazed the people of Katsina that ever afterwards they spoke of them as models to be followed.

When Songhay began to decline after a crushing defeat by Moroccan forces in 1592, the rulers of Kanem-Borno exerted increasing pressure on Hausaland from the east. According to Hogben and Kirk-Greene, "Every king of Katsina on his accession was required to send 100 slaves to the Mai of Ngazargamu and this tribute continued till the reign of Agwaragi in 1784. A similar tribute was exacted from Gobir."

While they were coping with outside forces, the Hausa states were also battling one another for supremacy in the region. Kano and Katsina, rivals for the bulk of the trans-Sahara trade, were often at war with one another, and both were at various times harassed by raiders from Kwararafa. The conflict between Kano and Katsina began late in the 15th century and went on for more than 200 years, ending with a peace treaty signed in 1706. On one occasion during the early 17th century, Kano's sarki Muhammad Zaki led a surprise attack on Katsina at the end of Ramadan, the month of fasting and prayer observed by all Muslims. In the words of the *Kano Chronicle*, "The men of Katsina came out to battle before the hour of the feast [the *K'aramar salla*, which marks the breaking of the fast]. The battle took place at Garaji. The men of Kano defeated the men of Katsina. The men of Katsina dispersed and fled, and the Kanawa took much spoil. They took four hundred horses, and sixty suits of horse armor. No one knows the amount of spoil or the number of the slain." This victory helped to erase the painful memory of an earlier battle during the 1570s, when all but three Kano attackers had disgracefully turned tail, leaving their outraged sarki virtually alone on the battlefield.

Feats of arms captured the imagination of the chroniclers, but Hausaland was essentially a peaceful and prosperous territory whose cities and towns were linked by numerous trade networks through which the goods of the world flowed with great regularity. Heinrich Barth, who traveled through the Sudan during the mid-19th century, was struck by the beauty and tranquillity of the Hausa countryside and was especially impressed by the vitality of Kano, then a city of about 30,000 inhabitants: "It was a very fine morning, and the whole scenery of the town in its great variety of clay

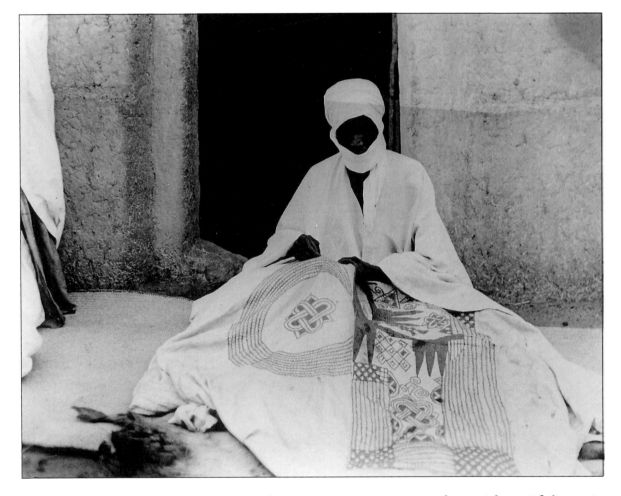

A Hausa embroiderer displays his handiwork. Growing a plentiful supply of cotton on their farms, the Hausa developed a large-scale textile industry that included weaving, dyeing, and embroidery.

35

houses, huts, sheds, green open places affording pasture for oxen, horses, camels, donkeys, and goats, . . . deep hollows containing ponds over-grown with the water-plant, . . . pits freshly dug up to form the material for some new buildings, various and most beautiful specimens of the vegetable kingdom, particularly the fine symmetric gónda or papaya, the slender date-palm, the spreading alléluba, and the majestic rími or silk cotton-tree (*Bombax*)—the people in all varieties of costume, from the naked slave up to the most gaudily dressed Arab—all formed a most animated and exciting scene."

In every Hausa city, the marketplace was the focus of social life, a spectacle of intense activity between sunrise and sunset every day of the week. As the British traveler Hugh Clapperton noted when he visited Kano in the 1820s, the principal medium of exchange in Hausaland was the cowrie, a small white shell harvested in the Indian Ocean and imported to the Sudan from North Africa. At the time, the rate of exchange was 2,000 cowries to a silver dollar, and Clapperton was amazed by the ability of the local merchants to accurately count out thousands of cowries in a short time. He also remarked upon the abundance and variety of goods and the careful organization of the market:

> Particular quarters are appropriated to distinct articles; the smaller wares being set out in booths in the middle, and cattle and bulky commodities being exposed to sale in the outskirts of the market-place: wood, dried grass, bean straw for provender, beans, Guinea corn, Indian corn, wheat, &c. are in one quarter; goats, sheep, asses, bullocks, horses, and camels, in another; earthenware and indigo in a third; vegetables and fruit of all descriptions, such as yams, sweet potatoes, water and musk melons, pappaw fruit, limes, cashew nuts, plums, mangoes, shaddocks, dates, &c., in a fourth, and so on. . . . The interior of the market is filled with stalls of bamboo, laid out in regular streets. . . . Bands of musicians parade up and down to attract purchasers to particular booths. Here are displayed coarse writing paper, of French manufacture, brought from Barbary [North Africa]; scissors and knives, of native workmanship; crude antimony and tin, both the produce of the country; unwrought silk of a red color, which they make into belts and slings, or weave in stripes into the finest cotton tobes [loose-fitting robes]; armlets and bracelets of brass; beads of glass, coral, and amber; finger rings of pewter, and a few silver trinkets; . . . pieces of Egyptian linen, checked or striped with gold; sword blades from Malta, &c., &c. . . . The market is regulated with the greatest fairness, and the regulations are strictly and impartially enforced.

Among the most important Hausa products were leather goods of all varieties (made from the hides of the ever abundant livestock) and dyed cotton cloth. As cotton grew so profusely in the fields, many Hausa families were engaged in the trade of weaving on hand looms. Dyeing, on the other hand, was performed in specialized workshops. Here, undyed garments were placed in large clay pots nine feet deep and three feet across and allowed to soak in a solution made from the stalks of the indigo plant. After three or four days, the garments were sent to a cloth glazer, whose workers placed them between mats and pounded them with wooden mallets until they took on an attractive gloss. A finished tobe, including dyeing, was sold for 5,000 cowries; the price of a *turkedi,* a long, loose-fitting woman's dress that tied in the back, varied from 2,000 to 3,000 cowries.

Heinrich Barth estimated that Kano exported more than 300 camel loads of cloth to Timbuktu each year, at a value of 60 million cowries, or 30,000 silver dol-

Following a centuries-old tradition, a group of wandering musicians perform in Kano's Kurmi Market. The musicians are available for hire by merchants, and their songs extol the virtues of the merchants' goods.

38

This intricately woven robe exemplifies the quality of Hausa craftsmanship. In addition to their skill with textiles, the Hausa also excelled at leatherwork.

lars. Reflecting on the extent and organization of Hausa textile production, Barth stated, "If we consider that this industry is not carried on here, as in Europe, in immense establishments, degrading man to the meanest condition of life, but that it gives employment and support to families without compelling them to sacrifice their domestic habits, we must presume that Kanó ought to be one of the happiest countries in the world."

In addition to their skill with cloth and leather, the Hausa were also exceptional builders and architects. In addition to the massive city walls, which could measure as much as 40 feet in thickness at the base, the Hausa built dwellings and mosques that were noted for their engineering and design. The Hausa had long been masters at constructing smooth and sturdy walls from mud mixed with vegetable matter and the blood of oxen. When this skill was augmented by techniques and materials imported from North Africa, Hausa architecture took on a new dimension. As Richard W. Hull has explained in *African Cities and Towns Before the European Conquest*,

> Burnt bricks (sun dried in the western Sudan, kiln dried in the central Sudan) made it easier to construct rectangular buildings with stronger,

more durable walls that permitted multistory construction. The walls of mosques [Muslim houses of worship] and chiefly homes could now support heavy flat clay roofs and even domes. The importation of termite-resistant palm timbers . . . enabled the Hausa to construct domes and clay roofs of almost monumental dimensions. . . . Domes of an extraordinary symmetry were constructed, despite the fact that builders possessed no rule, level, plumb, or blueprints. These structures, with their high vaulted ceilings, imparted an exhilarating sense of inner space. Outside, an area surrounding the dome was defined by delicate spires at the four corners of the building.

Though the history of Kano has been more carefully recorded, up until 1800 Katsina was the driving force in the development of Hausa culture. As Hogben and Kirk-Greene have written, "The old wealth and tradition of learning of Songhay became diverted her way, so that Katsina found herself a city of wide repute, a conscious apostle of civilization. Scholars now found their way to Katsina instead of to Timbuktu as of old. . . . Her citizens were renowned for their manners and courtesy, her schools for their learning, her administration and judiciary for their wisdom."

However, the traditions of Katsina also relate a disturbing incident that took place at the opening of the 19th century. At this time, the sarki of Katsina, Bawa dan Gima, decided to open a sacred house that the Katsina elders had sealed with red leather for hundreds of years. As Hogben and Kirk-Greene narrate the events, "Any king who opened this 'seat of power' would bring doom to his people by war. Thousands of egrets (*balbela*) flew out and filled the whole town. Shortly after the Fulani were astir with rumors of a religious war." The religious war that followed was to change the history of Hausaland.

39

Chapter 5 | JIHAD

The storm that was to sweep Hausaland during the 19th century did not arise among the Hausa themselves but among the Fulani migrants who had settled in the Hausa states. The Fulani were nomads, or wandering herders, who were descendents of both the Berbers of North Africa and the black peoples of the Sudan. Originally, the Fulani lived in the northwestern Sudan, in and around the kingdom of Takrur. The ruler of Takrur adopted Islam early in the 11th century, and the Fulani became Muslims at that time. During the following centuries, the Fulani had spread throughout the Sudan as they sought the best pasturelands for their herds of goats and cattle. Wherever they went, they lived in the rough-hewn style of the desert tribes and maintained a fierce attachment to Islam.

During the 15th century, a number of Fulani entered Hausaland from the Niger region in the West, in part to escape the wrath of the Songhay ruler Sunni Ali, who appears to have done his best to exterminate them. By the 18th century, the Fulani were so well established in the state of Gobir that some of their clans had abandoned the nomadic way of life and were living in permanent settlements. One of these settled clans, the Torodbe, formed a scholarly and religious elite among the Fulani. As staunch Muslims, the Torodbe objected strenuously to the form of Islam practiced by most of the Hausa rulers. They were especially offended by the mixing of Islamic observances with traditional beliefs, a custom long sanctioned both by Hausa rulers and by local Muslim teachers.

A 19th-century engraving depicts an attack on a fortified settlement. The war between the Hausa rulers and the Fulani Muslims, which lasted from 1804 to 1812, drastically altered the history of Hausaland.

41

Perhaps because of the stringent demands it makes on worshipers, the religion of Islam has given rise to reform movements such as the Torodbe almost from the start. In a number of cases, the reformers rose up and overturned regimes that they considered lax and immoral. Such actions were sanctioned by the Islamic doctrine of jihad, or "holy war," which allowed and even obliged Muslims to take up arms against unbelievers—even those who professed to follow Islam.

The Torodbe leader who inspired and led the jihad in Hausaland was Usuman dan Fodio (pronounced OO-su-mon dahn FOH-dyo). Born in 1754, Usuman was the son of a scholar and religious leader and was thought to possess supernatural powers even as a child. After he emerged as a religious leader in his

42

An encampment of Muslim nomads in the West African savanna, as depicted in an 18th-century engraving. The Fulani, a prominent nomadic group, began to pasture their herds in Hausaland as early as the 15th century.

own right, he became known to his followers simply as the Shehu. (The Hausa term *shehu* derives from the Arabic word *sheik* and literally means "teacher"—it is widely used as a title of respect among Muslims.) After living as a traveling preacher for many years, the Shehu became convinced that Islam could not be reformed in Hausaland by mere persuasion. In his view, the Hausa leaders had perverted the worship of Islam to such an extent that they qualified as unbelievers. In one of the mystical experiences he reported in his writings, the Shehu saw himself in the presence of al-Jilani, a deceased religious leader, who told him how to proceed: "He girded me with the Sword of Truth, to unsheathe it against the enemies of God."

In their intensifying campaign against the Hausa leaders, the Shehu and his followers appealed to more than just devout Muslims. Because they attacked luxury and injustice as well as religious laxity, the reformers made recruits in the lower orders of Hausa society. In many Hausa states, the common people were accustomed to paying high taxes that supported the lavish habits of the sarkuna. Corrupt government officials were known to confiscate livestock and other goods or to carry off young women to stock the

43

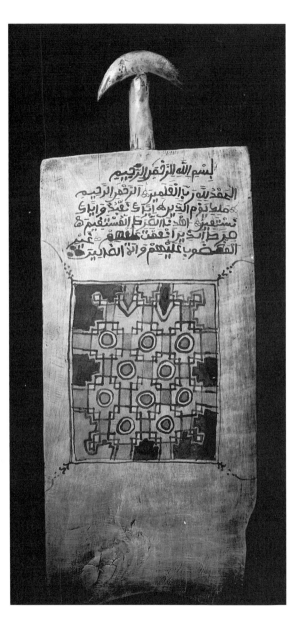

A wooden board from Hausaland contains a Koranic text in the ajami *script. After the triumph of the Fulani jihad in 1812, the great majority of Hausaland's inhabitants adopted Islam.*

sarkunas' harems. Thus, many Hausa had little reason to support the existing order; though they may have cared little for the strict religious principles of the Torodbe, they were willing to cast their lot with anyone who promised change.

The jihad finally erupted on the plains of Gobir in June 1804, following a long and bitter conflict between the Shehu and Sarki Yunfa. At the outbreak of the war, Yunfa's forces were superior in numbers and armaments, which included muskets imported from Europe. Not surprisingly, the Gobirawa were confident that they would quickly put down the Fulani uprising. In his book *The Sword of Truth,* Mervyn Hiskett has described the Gobirawa as "a colorful cavalcade, with the cavalry in their gay saddle-cloths, their plumed helmets, and their long lances couched." At first, Hiskett writes, the Gobirawa "treated campaigning as a picnic and carried large quantities of luxury foods, while numerous concubines accompanied their baggage train."

However, as the Hausa were fond of saying, "Even chain mail will not keep out the arrow of destiny." The confidence of the Gobirawa was quickly shattered at the Battle of Lake Kwotto, where the outnumbered jihadists withstood an all-out cavalry charge and then got the best of the Gobirawa in fierce hand-to-hand fighting, forcing their adversaries to flee in panic. This shocking defeat caused the rulers of the other Hausa states to unite against their common foe. The jihad then became a long, drawn-out struggle. Both sides endured punishing defeats; but as the war went on, the Muslims gradually gained in strength. In October 1808, Muslim forces stormed Alkalawa, the capital of Gobir, and killed Sarki Yunfa. This victory turned the tide, even though fighting continued for some time in other parts of Hausaland. By 1812, the victory of the reformers was assured.

Following his hard-fought triumph, the Shehu changed the name of Gobir to Sokoto, and there he established the seat of his new government, the Sokoto Caliphate. He placed half of Hausaland under the control of his brother Abdullah Muhammad and the other half under the control of his son Muhammad Bello—it was they who had led the Fulani forces in combat while the aging Shehu had devised the general strategy of the war. After the Shehu died in 1817, Abdullah ceded control of Sokoto to his nephew, who ruled effectively until his own death in 1837.

The reformers had intended to create the ideal Muslim state, one that would

(Continued on page 49)

44

SCENES OF HAUSA LIFE

Centuries ago, Hausa traders began plying West Africa's far-flung trade routes, often settling in the regions they visited. As a result, Hausa is now one of the two most widely spoken languages in Africa, along with Swahili. In addition to Hausaland itself, which includes northern Nigeria and part of the Niger Republic, Hausa communities can be found in such nations as Sierra Leone, Ghana, Cameroon, Chad, Gabon, Zaire, and Sudan.

The remains of a Hausa gateway in Zinder. The building of city walls in Hausaland was a massive undertaking that involved the entire community. When the sarki of Surame constructed the city's mud walls during the 16th century, a human chain of 10,000 people transported water in leather buckets from the Kebbi River.

Hausa herders tend to their cattle outside a village in the Niger Republic. In this region of Hausaland bordering on the Sahara Desert, rainfall is not sufficient for successful farming. With the aid of government-sponsored irrigation projects, the Hausa have concentrated on raising livestock.

Hausa women selling peanuts in a Niger marketplace. The peanut plant, native to South America, was introduced into Africa by Europeans. The plant grows especially well in tropical soils, and its edible seeds have been a major crop in West Africa since the 19th century.

In Sokoto, Nigeria, the market supervisor (wearing an indigo robe) greets the leader of an incoming caravan. As in centuries past, salt remains a highly prized commodity—the small pillar of salt in the foreground draws attention to the booth of a salt vendor.

(Continued from page 44)

strictly follow the commandments of the Koran and practice absolute justice. They achieved many of their goals. For example, the rulers of Sokoto freed large numbers of slaves as a reward for the slaves' support during the jihad, and a number of former slaves found themselves filling important government offices. And as the British scholar Murray Last has written, "The real achievement of the administrations after c. 1820 was their success in bringing back to the region a stabilty that was the foundation for an unprecedented economic boom, a period of growth not seen in the region since the fifteenth or sixteenth centuries."

However, the achievement of absolute justice is not often within the powers of ordinary mortals; Abdullah in particular complained bitterly about corruption and lax morals in the ranks of his officials. Nevertheless, the reform movement permanently changed the political face of Hausaland. In place of the individual fortress kingdoms, the Fulani established a strong centralized government. The ca-liph, who headed the government, was assisted by a vizier, or chief minister. The various regions of the caliphate were each headed by an emir. Each of the emirs reported to an official known as the *ko'fa* ("the door") who acted as an intermediary between the emirates and the vizier.

Of course, the Fulani were still a minority in Hausaland, and their reforms did not eradicate centuries of tradition. For example, many officials still used their traditional Hausa titles, and the people of Kano continued to play their long trumpets. However, the reformers had a powerful impact. Before the jihad, Islam had been confined to the Hausa cities, but it now began to spread among the people of the countryside. The art of writing the Hausa language in Arabic script also developed greatly through the efforts of Muslim schools, and a large body of Hausa proverbs, stories, and historical chronicles were now preserved in writing. The unity gained by the Hausa through these intellectual pursuits was to prove valuable in the trials that lay ahead.

49

Chapter 6 | THE ELEPHANT'S FOOTPRINT

Attended by a group of aides, the new emir of Katsina strides into the city's mosque following his installation in 1944. At this time, the British were in control of Hausaland; in addition to following all the traditional Hausa procedures, the emir was obliged to swear allegiance to the king of England.

With their sophisticated grasp of business and politics, the Hausa had always understood the influence of power and wealth in human affairs. Among their proverbs were such observations as "The elephant's footprint obliterates the camel's" and "The handsome man is king until the rich man appears." As much as any people in Africa, they understood the new pressures being exerted on the continent's way of life during the 19th century.

By the 1880s, the Sokoto Caliphate was threatened by the ambitions of Europeans, who had begun a large-scale slave trade along the coast of West Africa during the 16th century. The slave trade had been officially ended during the 19th century, but in 1870, the major European powers agreed to carve up Africa into colonies. At first, the British attempted to gain control over Hausaland by persuading local leaders to sign trade agreements. But, as the Germans and French began moving into the region, the British resorted to military force.

British troops successfully invaded Nupe in 1897 and Ilorin the following year. The Senegalese historian M. Gueye has described the ensuing action: "Surprisingly, other rulers of the north were not intimidated by these victories. On the contrary, apart from that of Zaria, all the other emirs, spurred on by their implacable hatred of the infidel [non-Muslims], were determined to die rather than surrender their land and faith. The British therefore had to launch a series of campaigns—against Kontagora in 1900, Adamawa in 1901, Bauchi in 1902, and Kano, Sokoto and Burwuri in 1903. The rulers of all these emirates rose to the occasion but they had no effective answer to their enemies' Maxim guns, rifles and muzzle-loading 7-pounder cannon and therefore suffered defeat."

Once the British were in control, they developed a system known as indirect rule. They allowed the Muslim emirates of Hausaland to remain intact and incorporated them into a new colony called Nigeria. The British promised not to interfere with the practice of Islam in the emirates as long as the emirs cooperated with the colonial government, which was located in Lagos, in southern Nigeria. (In the South, by contrast, Christian missionaries were given free rein and converted many Africans to Christianity.) Because of the policy of indirect rule, the political structure and the culture of Hausaland underwent little change even during the period of foreign domination.

When Nigeria gained its independence from Britain in 1960, it quickly emerged as the most populous and economically powerful of the new African nations. The emirates of the North now had a status comparable to the states of the United States, each controlling its internal affairs but also assuming rights and responsibilities as members of the Federal Republic of Nigeria. Because

northern Nigeria had been somewhat isolated from the South during the colonial period, Hausaland and its neighbors, such as the province of Borno, had not experienced as much economic development as had southern Nigeria. However, when Nigeria became one of the world's leading oil exporters during the 1960s and 1970s, the North gained a greater share of the nation's wealth.

Though the 20th century has brought many changes to Hausaland, tradition is still powerful in such states as Kano, Katsina, Zaria, Kebbi, and Sokoto, in which the emir is still the official head of an Islamic government. Kano, for example, is now the largest city of northern Nigeria, with a population of more than 500,000. Kano is in most ways a highly modern city, with a bustling business section and up-to-date transportation. At the same time, sections of the old city walls are still standing. Within the old city, the Kurmi Market, the emir's palace, the central mosque, and the old dyeing pits are still flourishing as they did centuries ago. Zaria, the former realm of Queen Amina, is now the intellectual center of Hausaland, with Ahmadu Bello University one of Africa's main centers of learning. But nowhere, perhaps, do the traditions of Hausaland enjoy such vi-

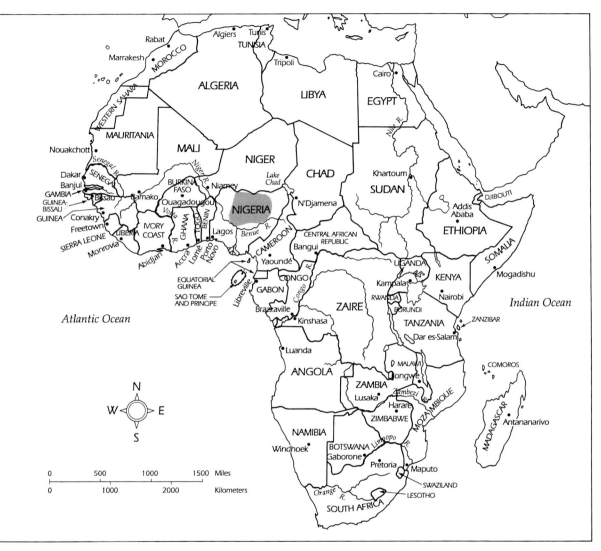

A map of present-day Africa. The shaded area indicates the territory of Hausaland, which now comprises the northern part of Nigeria, black Africa's most populous and prosperous nation.

brant life as in Katsina, Kano's old rival. The *K'aramar salla,* one of the most striking examples of the vitality of Hausa culture, is still performed faithfully at the end of Ramadan. L. Lewis Wall, a scholar studying the traditional healing

54

Resplendent in their armor and plumage, Hausa cavalrymen take part in a holiday celebration. As in centuries past, the Hausa continue to cherish their horses; one of their time-honored proverbs maintains that "an old horse is better than a new pair of shoes."

practices of the Hausa, has described the conduct of the ceremonies during the 1980s:

> Once the communal prayers have been performed an enormous procession forms. . . . The procession winds its way around the old city walls of Katsina and through the streets, amidst the cheers and applause of the masses of Hausa spectators jammed on the roadsides and lining all the rooftops. . . . Noble after noble passes by with his followers: hordes of dancers in green with feathers, mounted horsemen clad in orange, troops of turbaned swordsmen in flowing robes, and finally, bringing up the rear, the emir of Katsina himself, clad in brilliant white, riding a dark horse and protected from the mounting heat of the sun by a richly ornamented red-and-yellow parasol carried by an attendant, and followed by his guard of mounted spearmen, drummers on camels, and ceremonial cavalry. . . . The emir enters the parade ground and mounts to the reviewing stand, where from his position of command he receives the *jafi*— a succession of massed cavalry charges by the chiefs from each district with their subordinate village headmen and retainers, who pull their mounts up short and salute in front of the stand.

On one such occasion in the past, Katsina was attacked by the horsemen of Kano. Today, the Hausa have taken to heart the words of their old proverb, "Better live at peace than at palace." As Nigerians strive to create an example of democracy and prosperity for the continent of Africa, Hausaland's 1,000-year history of achievement offers a great source of pride and inspiration.

CHRONOLOGY

c. 2500 B.C.	Lake Chad begins to shrink during prolonged dry period; ancestors of the Hausa people move west in search of farmland
c. A.D. 1000	Fortified city-states begin to emerge in Hausaland; Bagauda begins reign as first sarki of Kano
1136–94	Tsaraki rules as sarki of Kano and completes the protective wall around the city; trade relations with North Africa begin
1145–95	Katsina emerges as a major power under the rule of Sarki Muhammad Korau
1290–1307	Shekkaru reigns as sarki of Kano; Islam begins to make its influence felt in Hausaland
1349–58	Reign of Yaki in Kano; Islam becomes the official religion of Kano's domains
1438–52	Sarki Abdullah Burja opens trade route between Kano and the southern forest belt; establishes Kurmi Market; introduces quilted armor and chain mail for cavalry; Kano's wealth increases dramatically
1463–99	Muhammad Rumfa increases the splendor of Kano's royal court and makes many innovations in government

1576–1610	Queen Amina of Zaria wages military campaigns throughout Hausaland and extends Zaria's borders into Nupe and Kwararafa; Gobir, Rano, Zamfara, and Kebbi emerge as powerful states
15th–17th centuries	Hausaland comes under pressure from Songhay to the west and Kanem-Borno to the east; several Hausa states are forced to pay tribute to foreign rulers; Hausa states, especially Kano and Katsina, battle among themselves for control of trade routes
late 18th century	Muslim reform movement begins among Fulani herders in northwestern Hausaland
1804	Led by Shehu Usuman dan Fodio, Muslim reformers launch "holy war" against the state of Gobir; gain dramatic victory at the Battle of Lake Kwotto
1908	Muslim forces capture Alkalawa, capital of Gobir, and kill Sarki Yunfa
1812	Muslims achieve final victory; Shehu establishes Sokoto Caliphate to govern Hausaland, which enjoys a new period of peace and prosperity
1897–1903	British forces complete conquest of Hausaland and create the colony of Nigeria.
1960	Nigeria gains independence and emerges as black Africa's most populous and prosperous nation; Hausa states become part of the Federal Republic of Nigeria

FURTHER READING

Adamu, Mahdi. *The Hausa Factor in West African History.* Zaria, Nigeria: Ahmadu Bello University Press, 1978.

Africanus, Leo. *History and Description of Africa.* 3 vols. Reprint of 1661 ed. New York: Hakluyt Society/Burt Franklin, n.d.

Ajayi, J. F. Ade, and Michael Crowder, eds. *History of West Africa.* 2 vols. New York: Columbia University Press, 1973.

Barth, Henry. *Travels and Discoveries in North and Central Africa in the Years 1849–1855.* 3 vols. New York: Harper & Brothers, 1857.

Clapperton, Hugh. *Narrative of Travels and Discoveries in Northern and Central Africa.* London: John Murray, 1831.

Davidson, Basil. *Africa in History.* Rev. ed. New York: Collier, 1991.

———. *The African Genius.* Boston: Little, Brown, 1969.

Davidson, Basil, with F. K. Buah and the advice of J. F. A. Ajayi. *A History of West Africa, 1000–1800.* New rev. ed. London: Longman, 1977.

Hiskett, Mervyn. *The Sword of Truth: The Life and Times of the Shehu Usuman dan Fodio.* 2nd ed. Evanston, IL: Northwestern University Press, 1994.

Hodgkin, T. H. *Nigerian Perspectives: An Historical Anthology.* Oxford: Oxford University Press, 1975.

Hogben, S. J., and A. H. M. Kirk-Greene. *The Emirates of Northern Nigeria.* London: Oxford University Press, 1966.

Hull, Richard W. *African Cities and Towns Before the European Conquest.* New York: Norton, 1976.

Johnston, H. A. S. *A Collection of Hausa Stories.* Oxford: Clarendon Press, 1966.

Moughtin, J. C. *Hausa Architecture.* London: Ethnographica, 1985.

Palmer, H. R. *Sudanese Memoirs.* London: Cass, 1967. (Includes the *Kano Chronicle.*)

Park, Mungo. *Travels in the Interior Districts of Africa.* Reprint of the 1799 edition. New York: Arno Press/New York Times, 1971.

Rattray, R. S. *Hausa Folklore.* 2 vols. Reprint of 1913 ed. New York: Negro University Press, 1969.

Sutton, J. E. G. "Towards a Less Orthodox History of Hausaland." *Journal of African History,* 20 (1979): 179–201.

Trimingham, John S. *A History of Islam in West Africa.* London: Oxford University Press, 1962.

———. *Islam in West Africa.* Oxford: Clarendon Press, 1959.

UNESCO General History of Africa. 7 vols. Berkeley: University of California Press, 1981–92.

Wall, L. Lewis. *Hausa Medicine.* Durham, NC: Duke University Press, 1988.

Webster, J. B., and A. A. Boahen, with M. Tidy. *The Revolutionary Years: West Africa Since 1800.* New ed. London: Longman, 1980.

GLOSSARY

archaeology   the study of the physical remains of past human societies

banza bakwai   the secondary Hausa states, according to Hausa tradition: Kebbi, Zamfara, Gwari, Kwararafa, Yoruba, Nupe, Yawuri

caliphate   an influential Muslim state ruled by a caliph, who is considered to be a successor of Muhammad

emirate   a state in Asia, Africa, or the Middle East governed by an independent Muslim chief, or emir

hausa bakwai   the original seven Hausa states, according to Hausa tradition: Daura, Kano, Zaria, Katsina, Gobir, Rano, Garun Gabas

indigo   a plant common in Hausaland that yields a blue dye; heavily used in the Hausa textile industry

Islam   the religion based upon worship of Allah and acceptance of Muhammad as His prophet

jihad   Arabic term meaning "effort"; developed into the concept of "holy war," the obligation of Muslims to defend Islam against unbelievers and expand its influence

K'aramar salla	ceremony following the end of the Ramadan fast in Hausaland, marked by processions and cavalry displays
kola	a West African nut valued for its stimulant properties
Koran	the holy book of Islam
lifidi	quilted body armor used to protect the horses of the Hausa cavalry
malam	a Muslim teacher and religious leader
mosque	a Muslim house of worship
Muslim	one who follows the religion of Islam
sarki	the traditional ruler of a Hausa city-state; plural *sarkuna*
shehu	a title of respect used for Muslim leaders in Hausaland; derives from *sheik*, an Arabic word meaning "teacher"
Sudan	the region of sub-Saharan Africa stretching from the Atlantic coast to the valley of the Nile River; derives from *Bilad al-Sudan,* Arabic for "land of the black peoples"
tobe	a loose cotton garment traditionally worn by the Hausa
turkedi	a traditional Hausa woman's garment, which reaches the ankles and ties in the back; usually dyed with indigo

INDEX

63

PHILIP KOSLOW earned his B.A. and M.A. degrees from New York University and went on to teach and conduct research at Oxford University, where his interest in medieval European and African history was awakened. The editor of numerous volumes for young adults, he is also the author of *El Cid* in the Chelsea House HISPANICS OF ACHIEVEMENT series and of *Centuries of Greatness: The West African Kingdoms, 750–1900* in Chelsea House's MILESTONES IN BLACK AMERICAN HISTORY series.

PICTURE CREDITS